Sang Kancil
and the
Farmer

by Jim Carrington

illustrated by Juanbjuan Oliver

 CAMBRIDGE
UNIVERSITY PRESS

 UCL
Institute of Education

There was once a clever mouse deer named Sang Kancil.

On the edge of the jungle was a garden filled with delicious fruit and vegetables.

The garden belonged to a grumpy farmer.

Sang Kancil often waited until the farmer went to work in the fields. Then he crept into the garden to help himself to the fruit and vegetables.

The farmer set traps in the garden, but Sang Kancil was too clever to get caught.

This made the farmer very angry. So he thought of a plan to keep his crops safe.

The next day, Sang Kancil crept quietly into the farmer's garden.

He was feasting on delicious berries when he heard a dog barking …

'RUFF! RUFF! RUFF!'

Sang Kancil jumped out of his skin. He tried to escape, but the dog grabbed his tail and wouldn't let go.

So Sang Kancil had to run away, leaving the end of his tail behind.

Sang Kancil had lost some of his tail, but he had learned a lesson. He must be cleverer than both the farmer and the dog from now on.

So he hid in the forest and watched until he noticed something important.

'Hmm,' said Sang Kancil to himself. 'Every day, just as the sun gets hot, the dog gets bored of guarding the crops and plods off to sleep in the shade.'

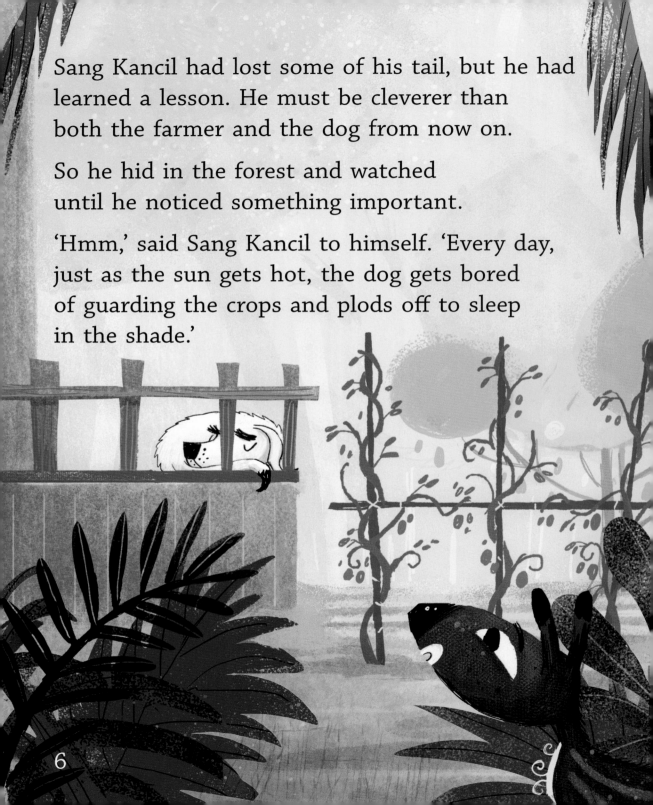

The very next day, as soon as the dog fell asleep, Sang Kancil filled his belly with the farmer's fruit.

The dog stayed fast asleep.

The farmer's crops were still disappearing.
He had to come up with a better plan.

He built a scarecrow. 'This will stop
the thieving pest,' he laughed.

8

The next morning, Sang Kancil crept out
of the forest as usual and darted into the garden.

The scarecrow was right in the middle
of the berry patch.

'Does the farmer think I'm stupid?' Sang Kancil
laughed. 'A scarecrow cannot stop me.'

He boxed the scarecrow with his hind legs.

But, oh ...

'I'm stuck!' cried Sang Kancil. 'The farmer has covered
the scarecrow with glue!'

When the farmer came back for his lunch, he locked Sang Kancil in a cage on the veranda.

'Ha ha. I've outsmarted you once and for all!' he chuckled.

'I'll deal with you when I've finished work.'

Sang Kancil tried to escape. He scratched at the cage door. He chewed at the bars. He rocked this way and that, hoping to knock the cage over. But all he did was wake the sleeping dog.

'Well, well, well. What have we here?'
yawned the dog, as he padded across the veranda.

'What does it look like to you?' replied Sang Kancil.

'It looks like the farmer tricked you, Sang Kancil,'
the dog said with a smile.

'You'll go in his cooking pot tonight.'

14

Sang Kancil gave a sly grin. 'Oh no, you're quite wrong,' he said.

'The farmer's keeping me safe to give to the king. The king wants a pet to treat like a prince!'

The dog was annoyed.

'That's not fair. I should live with the king.
I should be treated like a prince,' he said.
'Swap places with me.'

Sang Kancil shook his head. 'No, I won't.
I am going to live with the king.'

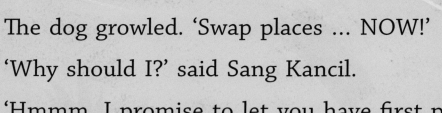

The dog growled. 'Swap places ... NOW!'

'Why should I?' said Sang Kancil.

'Hmmm. I promise to let you have first pick of the farmer's fruit,' replied the dog.

Sang Kancil pretended to think for a moment,
and then he grinned.

'It's a deal,' he said. 'Help me out of this cage.
We can change places ...'

Using his sharp teeth, the dog undid the bolt and opened the cage door.

Sang Kancil hurried out of the cage, and the dog rushed in. As quick as a flash, Sang Kancil slammed the door and bolted the cage shut.

'I tricked you, you silly dog,' laughed Sang Kancil.
'It looks like you'll be the one in the farmer's pot
tonight!'

And with that, he scurried away to feast
on the farmer's delicious berries.

23

Sang Kancil and the Farmer ● Jim Carrington

Teaching notes written by Sue Bodman and Glen Franklin

Using this book

Developing reading comprehension

This is a further adventure of the wily little mouse deer, Sang Kancil, who features in two other stories in Cambridge Reading Adventures (at Orange and Turquoise Bands). This story provides opportunity to build on the characterisation and plot developments seen in those books, although the story also stands alone as a traditional tale with all the features inherent in stories written in this style. At Gold Band, illustrations provide less support for the narrative, requiring greater inference on the part of the reader. Reading aloud is fluent and pacy to support comprehension across longer, more complex sentences, and reading can be silent.

Grammar and sentence structure

- Longer, more complex sentences use a range of punctuation devices: as, for example, on p.6.
- Sentence structure is varied to create effect, as in 'Using his sharp teeth, the dog undid the bolt …' (p.20).
- A range of grammatical conventions are used to move the story forward, such as personal reflection ('Hmmm,' said Sang Kancil to himself.' on p.6) and time connectives ('the very next day'; 'when the farmer came back for his lunch').

Word meaning and spelling

- Characterisation is portrayed through word choice and the interplay between characters through dialogue.
- Idiomatic language is used for effect: 'once and for all' (p.10); 'quick as a flash' (p. 21).
- Opportunity to read unfamiliar words on-the-run, using appropriate word-reading skills to solve them.

Curriculum links

Language development – Use drama strategies (such as role on the wall or hot-seating) to explore Sang Kancil's motives and actions. Transform the story, for example as a wanted poster for the capture of Sang Kancil, or a letter of apology from the dog to the farmer for letting the mouse deer escape.

Design & Technology – Devise other traps to catch Sang Kancil, but without harming him. These designs could then form the basis of an innovation on the story.

Learning outcomes

Children can:

- read with fluency and expression to aid comprehension
- take note of punctuation and sentence structure in longer, more complex sentences, to support fluent reading
- identify features of traditional tales in this retelling, and evaluate their effectiveness.

A guided reading lesson

Book Introduction

Note: Books at Gold Band may be too long for one guided reading lesson. This lesson plan assumes that children will have had some pre-reading activity to familiarise themselves with the first few pages, up to page 4.

Give each child a copy of the book. Ask them to tell you about what they have read. Establish the characters of Sang Kancil, the dog and the farmer, and what the children know already of Sang Kancil (that he is clever, and is hard to catch).

Orientation

Say: *So, Sang Kancil has lost his tail. But he still wants to find a way to eat the farmer's crops. Let's find out what happens next.*